We live again those happy days of yore
on campus, field, in classroom, dorm, at drill
                      Dr. John Ashton, Class of 1906

Published in the United States of America 2013
by The Latest Publications

204 A Fairview
College Station, TX 77840

Email: thelatestpublications@gmail.com

Design by: Robert Carpenter

Copyright Glenn Allen Phillips
Library of Congress
catalog card number applied for

No part of this book may be reproduced in any form, or by any means, without prior permission in writing from the publisher

ISBN: 978-0-9898516-0-2
Printed and bound in the U.S. by Bookmasters Ashland, OH

for Jeff Wetuski '91, the first Aggie I ever knew

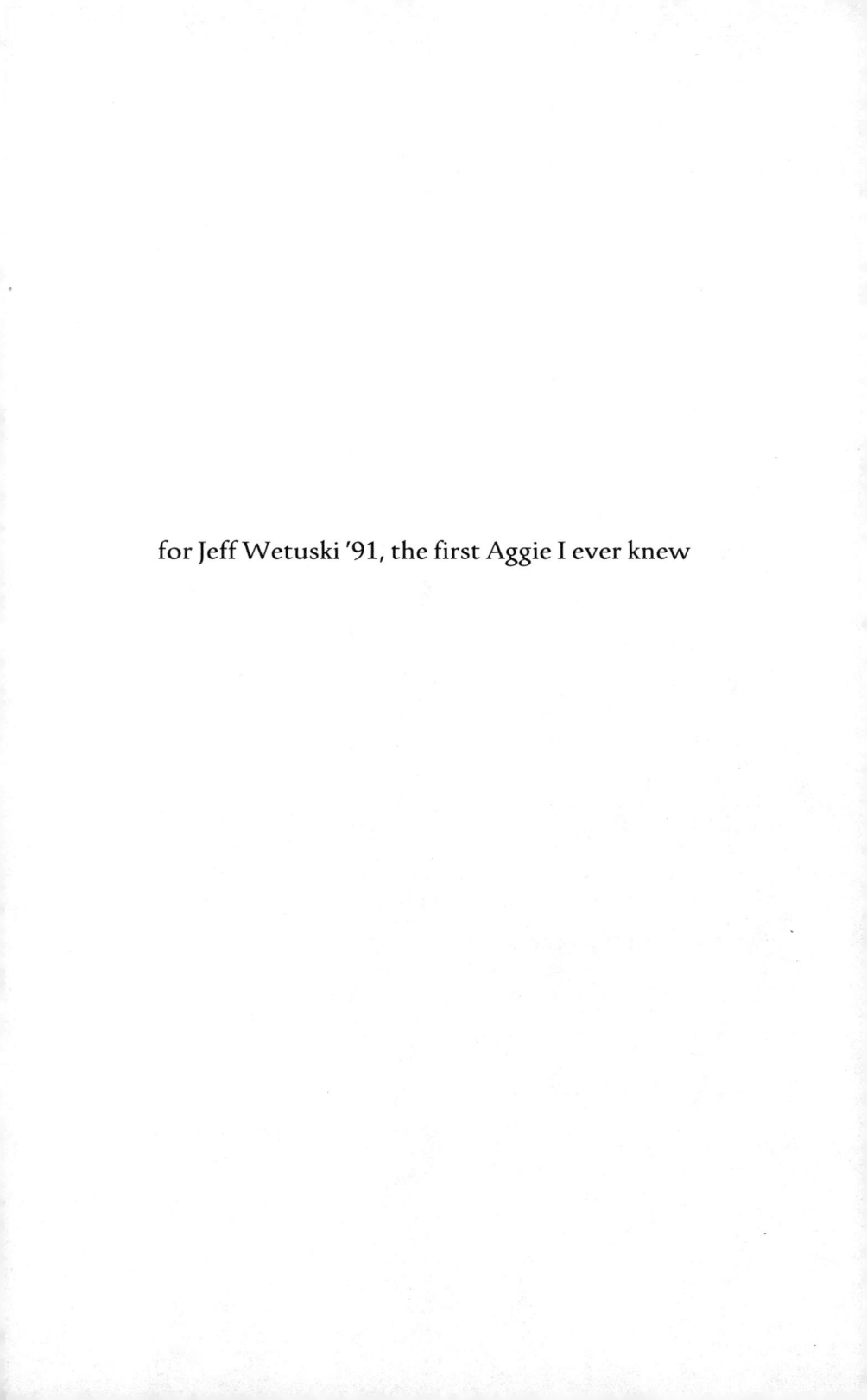

thanks to

Dr. Ron Richards '64 for encouraging me to apply to Texas A&M.

My parents for letting me go.

Fish Camp for making me stay.

Dr. Janet McCann for teaching me to be a poet.

Jason Chaka '02 for constantly encouraging both me and this project.

Kyle Woodruff '09 for always pretending to like my poetry.

Jon '09, Allison '10 and Donnie Quick '12 for advice and baking.

Aaron Forbis-Stokes '09 for being a kindred spirit.

Mr. and Mrs. Currie for offering a place to write.

Alejandra Merheb '01 for joining me in so many Aggie adventures.

Mark Charbonneau '01 and Michael Gerecke '02 for being great men.

Travis Endlsey '02, Scott Sharp '02, Kyle Setliff '01, Ricky Wood '01 and Tae Park '01 for helping me find something to say.

The men of the Lodge for being great friends.

The men of 1006 Holik for being a great family.

The Aggie Men's Club for making this place a home.

Dr. Ben Welch '90 for his ceaseless encouragement.

Dr. Yvonna Lincoln (my dissertation chair) for letting me leave.

Fellow Students
a collection of Aggie poetry by Glenn Allen Phillips '01

author's note

For many poets, their first book is a greeting. For me, this book is a way to say farewell.

Originally a small project in my master's program, I wanted to know if it were possible to capture the Aggie experience in poetry. Poetry is richer than prose, more resilient than stories and more versatile than photography. I wanted to know if it were possible to write a collection that a reader could read and subsequently understand what it means to be an Aggie. I now think the answer is "No." This book of poetry is unfortunately limited to its author's experiences. It cannot explain everything that makes Texas A&M University unique, at least in part because I still do not completely understand it.

All I can offer is what I have seen, felt, thought and imagined during my journey through these hallowed halls. These poems are not a complete picture of Texas A&M University. These poems are scattered snapshots. I hope they resonate within other Aggies that have, do or will call this place home.

Contents

| Introduction | 11 |

Campus
Stitched	15
Passing	16
College Station Sunset	17
The graduate	18
No food or drink allowed	19
Train	21
Open letter to James Earl Rudder	22
The day the wall came down	24
Spence Park lamp	25
Teacher and students	26
Decoration	27
If a tower falls...	28
The ant farm	29
The breezeway	30
MSC renovation	32
Campus visitors	33
A day in the Corps	34
Royalty	35
Observations	36
College Station, Texas	37
Walking at night	38

Classroom
| 14 students | 43 |
| Giants | 46 |

Graduation	47
Study carol	48
In memoriam: Douglas Brooks	49
Business	51
Developmental mathematics	53
How to teach in three easy steps	55
Turn of the century	56
Attendance policy	58
Why I am writing a dissertation about veterans	60
Waiting on a professor	61
Advice to students	62
Advice to teachers	63
On stage	64
Pedagogy	67

Traditions

There from here	71
Ringbearer	72
Bonfire villanelle	73
Greetings	74
Midnight Yell	75
The other education	76
Muster	78
Now forming	79
Century tree	81
Almost a century	82
Authority	84
The candle	85
Bonfire remembrance 2009	86
This Ring - a cinquain	87

Weight	88
Silver Taps revisited	95
Echo Taps	96
12th Man	97
The promise	98

My experience

My scrapbook	103
Writing process	104
About to leave these halls	105
Composites	106
Fellow students	108
Passing the torch	109
On turning 19	110
Waiting	112
Souvenirs	114
Close	115
Yesterday	117
Non-reg's lament	118
Preparation	119
Before the game	121
Simply put	122

Goodbye	124

Introduction

I didn't write this with pen and paper,
a ball point pigeon to carry my words.
I carved it in the wood of a bone
a bench, a low branch.
I painted it on the side of a barn
a bell, the meat of my hand.
I screamed it against a slow-moving train
matching her metal notes, wail for wail.

I didn't write this with pen and paper,
ink poured out like a lake.
I burned it into the earth,
stitched it in the sky.

My poems are not an echo;
they are the walls that send
my voice back to me.

Campus

Stitched

Come let me take you
on a tour of this
patchwork campus.

On thin threads
we will bob and
weave through the
fabric of this place.

I will show you
every stitch of a student,
every hem of tradition.

We will walk from
square to square
on needled legs,

sewing our colors,
picking up where others
left off.

And one day,
years from now,
reclining and still,
we will pull
this campus over our
cold bones

and be warmed
by its quilted memories.

Passing

I am content as I sit here
on the cold concrete of Albritton,
my back against a pillar.

The flag in front of the Academic Building
is not waving as much as it is
rocking, a gentle reminder it's alive.

The cars that pass and circle me
run through a small mirrored puddle
left by an afternoon rain.

I can't help but think, on days like this,
when campus is bare and crawling,
how much like a wind we are,

here as long as it takes to walk
barefoot on the grass, compose a sonnet or two,
then disappear from beneath the well-lit sky.

College Station sunset

I'm sure that somewhere
the sunset is better.

Somewhere the red
is nobler,

and the lengthy pink
straddles both sides of a cloud.

Somewhere the sun is sinking
into water or mountains or both,

balanced on a salty crest,
a shadowy slope of snow.

I'm sure that somewhere
the sunset is better.

But as I sit here in this summer breeze,
watching this sun slip behind a risen steeple,

as birds dart in and out
of it's glowing belly,

as the Crepe Myrtles
shake their embarrassment to the ground,

I can't help but think,
though others may be better,
this one is surely enough.

The graduate

Let me walk on the
thin ribbon of your
Möbius mind, and I,
a dangerous kind of
new, will defy the
tired cords of gravity
and stay suspended

here

in the airy jungle
of the unknown—
this lamp, my only
light.

A twisted head,
just the beginning.

Tomorrow, I will
twist your yesterdays
until you find
yourself,

upside-down and awake,
the only un-eaten apple
in a sea of falling floors.

No food or drink allowed

Do not bring food or drink into the library.
Sneak food or drink into the library.

Hide Jelly Beans between your toes
as you walk briskly past the doorman.

Wrap licorice in a tight rubberband
with your pen and pencils.

Slide taffy into the space
between your calculator and its cover.

Do not bring food or drink into the library.
Smuggle food or drink into the library.

Cut the meat out of a textbook
and replace it with a sirloin steak.

Slip sliced baby carrots
along the spiral of your notebook.

Fill every pocket of your backpack
with fresh fruit and whipped cream.

Do not bring food or drink into the library.
Secret food or drink into the library.

Place an avocado beneath your hat.
Spread *foie gras* between the pages of your books.

Walk into the foyer with a can of sardines,
Talking on it like a cell phone.

Comment on how hungry you are.

Do not bring food or drink into the library.
Sneak food or drink into the library.

Bring Nalgene bottles full of milk.
Pack your purse with pineapple juice.

Fill your mouth with red wine and
Walk through the revolving door
Puffy-cheeked and smiling.

Then, when no one is looking, enjoy
A picnic on the fourth floor.
Using Hemmingway as a plate

And Austen to wipe the corners of your mouth.

Train

There's silence before the train,
stretching like rubber bands,
cracks in the soundwalk.

Blinking red anticipation,
crossed arms wait impatiently
for cue.

When the whistle gapes
the sky shudders,
pushing us through a pin-hole.

My freshman year I jumped,
feeling the tracks rattle,
looking for a light.

The next year it sat still
between my ears,
rolling to fall out of conversation.

My junior year I don't remember
the train or my junior year
with its long lines.

My senior year the train whispered.
I heard it in the distance
some great lost whale
searching for an ocean.

Open letter to James Earl Rudder

And what of the wind
that snakes and spins
across this open field?

Do you hear it?

And what of the trees
that bend and gnarl
beneath the singing sun?

Do you see them?

And what of the buildings,
stone comrades,
standing ever ready?

Do you salute them?

And the students
that flood by you
like a slow brook,

and the faculty
that hurry past
in shoes of things to do,

and the other men
and women, just as still,
reflecting the same light,

do you know them?

And are their names,
just as ours, written
on the heavy pages

of the book you always hold?

The day the wall came down

I say go there at night. Go there when the wind is pulling on the galloping flags like so many small hands. I say go there when the lights are holding the statue, ten feet from the earth. Because it is then, in the calmest of moments, you see the horses for what they are — small beginnings of a storm.

When I was a freshman, the horses were new. The old people would come in droves holding their grandchildren like spaghetti, and offering them to the bronze gods. The old people knew the wall before it fell. The old people knew the horses.

Years later, I still go to the statue. A man now in a world of children, I sometimes take them with me. I hold them up to the steady eyes of the stallion, the steady eyes of the mares. I watch the wall fall in their reflective eyes.

I say. Go there at night. Go there when the wind is the only sound. Go there when you can softly hear the Berliners—their maddening cries of defeat, of victory.

Spence Park lamp

we all have our favorite places
the nooks and crannies of this campus
we sneak back to when
no one is looking

some climb
      roofs and trees
           just to be above it all
                  birds eyes and such

Some hide
      in hallways and alleys
           pushing against the walls
                blending into the architecture

some stand
      near statues and fountains
           displayed like a trophy
                a parade in repose

I sit on a bench and stare
at a lamp whose concrete concentric circles
makes me think, the rock
that was thrown is

paused

just inches beneath the ground

Teacher and students

High on the shoulders of imagination,
They reach with infinite arms
To scratch the floor of heaven.
Four children touch the sole of God
Tiptoed on the pages of their immortality.
They offer up the feather of a nearly wingless angel.

Knowing the treasure they seek,
She stands with careful eye,
Sacrificing herself to show them the way.

Decoration

How many students walked this seal
Looking forward, never down?
How many read it like a book,
When it was meant to be a crown?

If a tower falls...

Albritton Tower's falling down,
not brick by brick, but sound by sound.
It's all that we can do to keep
her heavy notes up off the ground.

Every hour on the hour,
you'll find us circled round her tower
with rakes to rake and brooms to broom
the notes the air does not devour.

We bag them up and tie them tight,
careful that the morning light
can't see the sounds we couldn't save
from hitting ground the previous night.

The only way she'll disappear—
a day when no one's here to hear.

The ant farm
for Jerod Brazeal '06

Driving down University
I can't help but stare
At its windowed walls,

Engineers scurrying frantically
Up and down its
Artificially well-lit halls,

Students impressively carrying
Over ten times their body weight
In theorems and chalk.

From the road they seem
completely unaware that I am outside
observing their every move,

That I am patiently
looking for their queen,

That I am counting
Their tunneled turns.

That I alone can
Save them from sandy oblivion.

The breezeway

Hold on tight;
these winds are
unforgiving.

Anchor yourself
with rocks,
small boulders
if possible.

Plant yourself
between bricks.
Deep roots yield
longevity.

Gather your friends
tight into a circle.
Tie arms like
shoelaces.
Double-knot
on stormy days,

Because,
these gales,
these gusts,
these zephyrs
are not here to cool you.

They're here to
tear you from the earth,
to pull you by the skin.

Sweep sand
and welcome
whomever comes next.

MSC renovation

But where will they put the spheres
while the living room is renovated?

Surely not in the building
as it bends and breaks and burns.

And surely not on display in
some unused hall or treeless arboretum.

No, I think they'll be stored away
in some tight-lipped closet about the city
where predictably one small boy
with a bobby pin and a bit of luck

will uncover the find of the century.

Two whole worlds, one blue, one red,
Being held, prisoner planets
in the dark.

Campus visitors

I hear the bells like I hear my mother's voice,
A soft reminder of her presence.

When the wind pushes leaves I see my grandfather
Dancing in blue jeans worn at the knees.

The bricks are rough but warm,
Patient like my father, not as strong.

The sunrise is my brother, a father himself,
Digging hands in the night to pull out day.

My sisters are a fountain and the rain,
Both trying to keep the ground soft, the air cool.

My middle brother is a statue, stronger than he thinks,
Golden in the light.

And I, I am probably just a bench
That was, is, or, perhaps, will be
Someone else's grandfather.

A day in the Corps

It's the hour the sun begins to whisper words of color,
uncovering Monets of blurry greens and greys.
As light stretches wide arms from the east,
spilling pink and orange into timid blue,
once sleepy buildings shake off fog and dew
reluctantly accepting their duty to wake.

It's the hour the sun hangs high like a trophy,
brick and mortar celebrating their stateliness,
walking proudly through meticulously manicured forests,
green woodlands flooded with concrete tributaries.
Statues aflame, illuminated with significance and sunlight,
answering in full attention to the commanding call of day.

It's the hour the sun retreats,
painting a dimming sky with soft color,
casting shadows across a watercolor canvas,
grey silhouettes against the daylight's last furies,
calming sharp corners and edges to blurs of dusk,
stepping out of formation, regressing to anonymity.

It's the hour the moon climbs into the sky,
bouncing its reflections through hollow halls.
Aluminum light pours through campus,
filling an ethereal city with time and fog,
with forgotten voices, with echoing footsteps.
The city torches paint the sky maroon.

Royalty

From the top of Harrington Tower,
just before the sun slips away,
the dome of the Academic Building
offers a subtle severity,
anachronistic on our clay-colored campus.

This little castle of a building,
with its windowed eyes and lattice balconies,
is not unlike one that some Renaissance
prince would step out onto, survey his land,
and walk back into his tapestried halls.

As I look down among
the grassy lawn of Cushing and through
the heavy boughs of the Century Tree,
I am not surprised to see
these regal students,

small kings and queens of
monarchies yet unmade.

Observations

They say if you sit on a bench,
this bench, you will see all
50,000 students on this campus.

I have counted 49,999.
Someone must be missing.

College Station, Texas

You can keep your windy cities
and pockets full of light,
your skyscrapers and office buildings
that stand like eager children.
You can keep your undergrounds
and asphalt spaghetti, the
commuters who ride them like
rollercoasters. You can keep your
elevators and moving sidewalks
your neon nights and midnight oil.

Just leave me this railroad town
with its slow summer clouds
and crawling heat. Leave me
its humble bones and modest homes.
Leave me its translucent stars
that stir and rise with the
faraway bellow of a southbound train.

Walking at night

I awoke last night
in a brilliant peace
and walked, bare-footed,
into the hot night air.

The stars, who have
always been for the poor,
spun around my outstretched
hand, and grabbing one,
I fell to my knees.

My unopened hand, still
an arm's length above my head,
a trembling fist, opened
like a hibiscus,

and for a moment, I
held both the sky and earth
at once.

Classroom

14 students

she sits sipping
coffee and Kafka,
meditating on both,
her legs folded beneath her
like origami.

he bends balsa wood
in another all-nighter.
pizza boxes and Red Bull
balanced perfectly
in a makeshift Parthenon.

he eyes the meniscus,
recording and reporting
repetitive reactions,
the whole while thinking
of stethoscopes and surgery.

he stands, head tilted,
staring at a blank wall,
determining where best to begin
in his inductive proof
that he exists.

she listens idly
to Lincoln and King,
spinning her pen,
biding time until

her presidency

she draws on graph paper,
hand meat green from ink.
she tic tac toe's between inventions,
all the while marveling
at her perfectly perpendicular x's.

he eats numbers like candy,
color coded, flavor filed
tax bracket candy,
and when he hiccoughs
he always counts until they stop.

she checks NASDAQ
at the Rec, climbing
in place, thinking how good
her calves will look in business casual,
her hair swept up in ambition.

she colors cardboard with map pencils,
talks about times tables and reading,
never once giving thought to those
who don't know, she's got the future
stuffed in her puff-paint pockets.

she cuts open cats,
smelling like formaldehyde,

making sure the organs stayed
in their proper place
so next time, she won't have to look.

he plays Rimsky-Korakov,
sending bumblebees afloat
from his black and white hive,
reading sheet music like novels,
where the wind gives ovations.

he's buried in the library,
counting Anne Boleyn's fingers
and Egypt's black obelisks.
he walks backwards,
glancing behind him to the future.

he waits for rain
like earth does, thirsty,
sinking hands into black soil,
pulling his grandfather
from a harvest ready belly

he swallows prayer beads,
watching Shiva stretch into an asterisk.
he chews on gospels
while he waits,
taking short breaths in Aramaic.

Giants
for Dr. Ron Richards '64

I walked here on the back of a man,
balanced on the bridge of his shoulders.
He unknowingly held my weight.

Then a child, all I offered was my thanks.

Now a man, I offer him my back,
strong and wide enough to carry those
whose weight he can no longer bear.

Stack them high about my neck.
Let them curl around my clavicles.
I have practice carrying heavy loads.
I learned to walk by watching giants.

Graduation

Somewhere in these names
there are mothers and pianists
and priests and beggars
and lawyers and criminals
and the best and the worst
of us. Somewhere
in these names there are
men clawing at the gates
and men hiding beneath the bed.
There are women arriving
and leaving,
and in the oceans of thin
black robes and stiff mortar boards,
the only difference from my mezzanine seat
is how the temperature has dropped
as they all hold their breath
at once.

Study carol

I sit beneath heavy chandeliers
and their over-sized lanterns
hoping some wandering student will
stop at the piano
and break the scholastic silence with a song.

A song buzzes just above the slippery booth
where my coffee cools
and the pancakes pass like heavy traffic,
where the syrup pours slowly
like the turning of these books.

These books surround me like an army,
standing at attention in their narrow ranks and files.
I lean back on my fourth floor seat
ready for the pending war,
Shelley pointing an innocent dagger at Shaw.

I read Shaw on the mountain of my bed,
balancing his leafy plays on my pillow.
The low light lulls me onto stage
where I suddenly awake to a young girl
sorting flowers where she sits.

In memoriam: Douglas Brooks

I was in one of your lecture classes.
three hundred students stacked like
dominoes in a classroom that once
belonged to Biology. You came in the
first day and wrote in frantic letters
"Country Matters." By the end of the
lecture you led us to worship at the womb
of an abstinent queen. So were the
wild adventures of all your students.

Almost a decade later, lining up
dominoes of my own, I can't help
but think of the electricity of it all,
how like lightning we were occasionally
struck. How for the rest of the
semester we would gather around the
tallest poles, hoping to be hit again.

I didn't get the chance to tell you,
so I'll say it in memoriam, but we're all
still here, penitent at your feet, quiet
for the next light that escapes your lips.

We have grown in number over
the years, not just adding by semester,
but recruiting beyond your classrooms.

We are now armed to the throat,
hungry for the moment when we, your
unexpected army, will turn this war around.

Business

I am sitting at an all-night restaurant,
hours into the hum of an early morning.

To my left, David is buried in annuities,
frantically calculating interest rates and dividends.

Across the table, Tyler is building a management project
like a model airplane, covered in data and epoxy.

At some distance I'm reading Billy Collins' new book of poems,
my chair leaned back on two unstable legs.

As I look over my glasses,
I can imagine David without his beard,
adjusting the rearview mirror on his Lexus,
Tyler pushing up the double-Windsor knot
of his red silk tie.

Part of me wants to become them,
to pry out their corporate bones,
rebuild myself in Armani,
and walk, leather-shoed,
through their cubicled labyrinth.

But the other part, stronger now,
wants instead to applaud them
with the thumbed pages of my book,

slip into a loose poem,
and breathe easy,

thankful that what they're doing
is none of my business.

Developmental mathematics

I teach developmental mathematics.
In the 1990s we would have called it
remedial. In the 1790s we would
have called it cutting edge.

My students are the leftover students.
I teach the prom queens who no longer
have a kingdom. I teach the tattooed
and the pierced. I teach the veterans
who always sit near the door.

My students are non-traditional students,
students who work "nine-to-fives"
students who have full-time lives,
students who leave my evening class
and stock the local grocery store until
the sun rises.

In my class we factor, distribute, solve,
and simplify. We do math that, for many,
was done alongside puberty.

My students did not get it, or, more often,
they were not given it. And so I hold
them by their mathematical hands,
and we walk into the world.

My students think they are stupid.
They have been told as much by faculty,
friends, family, and every news report that
compares America to China.

My students think that I am smart
because I can divide, multiply, add,
and subtract without so much as
moving a pencil.

Other people like that I teach developmental
mathematics. They say that I am a good soul.
They say that I should be lauded for my effort.

What they don't know is that one
by one I am building a small army.

What they don't know is that the
prom queen is about to find her crown.

What they don't know is that the
grocery store stocker just factored a trinomial
without so much as moving a pencil.

We're all climbing ladders here.
My money is on the ones who were told to stop
and kept climbing.

How to teach in three easy steps

1.
You must balance them
on your shoulders,
let them look past the
high fence you cannot.
You must trust their eyes
while yours squint and smile,
their heels planted
firmly in your neck.

2.
You must slip on their
hands like gloves,
and pull on their
legs like trousers.
You must ease into their
tight skin then
watch them move,
with you, pulsing at their wrists.

3.
You must give them
each a bite of your apple
then discuss its qualities
before you say it's red,
before you say it's sweet,
before you even conclude
that it's an apple.

Turn of the century
for Dr. Jerome Loving

This afternoon as I
Pulled my door shut
And prepared to walk
Down my office's
Windowless corridors,
I heard a tapping,

Not the slow methodical
Hum of the computer keys
Or the rhythmic scratching
Of pencil to paper,
But a deeper, intentional
Sound, almost violent.

Glancing down the smaller halls,
I saw a door barely open,
Light pushing its way out.
I pictured the man inside
With his ancient typewriter,
Balanced on biographies.

I wondered who,

One hundred years before,
Stood as I stood then,
Hearing some anachronistic sound.

Who, for a moment,
Straddled centuries
One hand heavy,
One hand light,
Slowly spinning towards the sun.

Attendance policy

Class will begin promptly
at 8:00 am every Monday,
Wednesday, and Friday.

Be in your seats with
paper and pen spread
like a breakfast table.

At 8:00 am, sharp, I will
begin by cracking the first
egg of conversation.

We will spend the next
50 minutes scrambling
for yolky truths.

If you are late, your
bits of egg will go
to another, hungrier student.

If you are absent we
will assume you are dead,
and, in mourning, will eat your egg.

If you return to us,
a prodigal pupil, we will,
in celebration, give you our eggs.

But, as a warning, if it
happens more than once,
we may begin to doubt
your resurrection.

Why I am writing a dissertation about veterans

For my students, the ones
that click their pens like
a detonator
the ones that can't fit
all of their life into my classroom

For the soldiers in unpronounceable places,
their ability to do
what I did not, could not
for the wind and the words
and the open-mouthed earth,

for those that came home
to banners, balloons, and babies
to an empty gate and a
lost bus ticket

for the day after the parade.

For the teachers who can't teach them
for the schools that can't fit them
for the students who were soldiers,

I am trying to open the windows.
I am trying to fill this place with light.

Waiting on a professor

He will not come,
not today.
I'm sure of it.

How could he come
when there are Alps
unexplored?

How could he come
with treasure hiding
beneath the ocean floor?

How could he come
with Amazonian tributaries
unaccounted for?

He will not come,
not today.
I'm sure of it,

not while kites sit windless,
not while surf begs at beaches,
not while climbable cliffs crumble,

not with my bed, so close, still warm.

Advice to students

Make mistakes, big heavy-handed mistakes.
Don't settle for outside of lines.
Aim for outside of dimensions.
Use indelible ink.
Sing out of tune.
Get lost.
Find yourself.
Hide yourself.
Count.

Eat berries from trees, the red ones,
the ones they warned you about.

Fall repeatedly, purposefully, infinitely
until you are confident you'll get up again.
Then, when sure the ground is forgiving,
climb to the highest branch and
jump.

Advice to teachers

Catch.

On stage
for Gary Wyatt and Lydia Miller-Wyatt

His hand shakes now
so that he cannot
hold his coffee.

His wife, elegant
and swift, has a thin
neck and holds

his coffee for him.
His students fail
to notice.

His students, queens
and priests, memorize
their lines like prayers

and worship, religious
fanatics that they are,
each night for hours.

He is not their god,
but he is their Platonic
shadow on the cave wall.

He is flawless and moves
the students like furniture,
like lions.

He has seen this before.
And in each young man
he sees a young Tybalt.

In each girl, a Juliet.
And in me, he saw Miller
and Shakespeare and

a promise that my best
was still in the wings.
And it has been years

since I last took the stage.
Both the lights and the
mechanics of the curtains

are strangers. But when
I hear the applause of my
typewriter keys, when I

see an ovation at the end
of every class, I always
look to the audience.

He is there, as he has
always been, an intensely
focused brow above

a widening smile. His wife,
with the thin neck, still holding
his trembling hands.

Pedagogy

We, teachers, want them, our students, to love us.
Not love us, adore us.
Not adore us, worship us.
We want them to worship us.
Have consensual, intellectual affairs with us.
Meet us on the redbrick street corners of the classroom.
Sit with us on chalk-dusted rose petals.
> Take moonlit walks under heavy fluorescent bulbs.

We, teachers, want them, our students, to talk about us in whispers.
We want them to write about us in sonnets,
Fourteen lines of us, rhyming,
> Shakespearean, Petrarchan, heroic, coupleted *en finale*,
> > Etched somewhere on warm pink marble.

We, teachers, want them, our students, to love us the same way
That we, students, love our teachers.
The same way that we walk with William in sylvan copse.
The same way that we stand beside Emily in her empty bedroom
The same way that we gladly oven our heads beside Sylvia
> Unconcerned with our gassy suicides.

Traditions

There from here

I put my penny at your feet,
in hopes that it would be enough
to buy a page in your history.

I tip-toed around your glass-sheet grass,
in hopes that my heels could press
more permanently into harder ground.

I stood screaming at your football games,
sure my voice would awaken the ghosts
sleeping beneath my feet.

I stood silent in your candlelight,
a sharp-collared suit and uncomfortable shoes,
vigilant and waiting for my name to be read.

I ate your lectures and listened to your pontificates,
knowing it was my responsibility to genuflect
at your be-booked and bending altar.

I held you in my hands, where I still hold you,
like water, like marbles, like ice,
not with ease, but by choice.

Ringbearer

There is a boy whose earliest memory
is a smooth gold band,
his grandfather's hand,
patting him on the chest.

Now almost a man,
his grandfather gone,
he keeps, in a box beneath his bed,
a tin-covered Bible
and the smooth gold band.

His own ring has an eagle, flags, and stars.
And each day he rubs them,
not nervously, but with patient plan;
to smooth himself into his grandfather.

Bonfire villanelle

There is no fire here, but I am warm.
Wind crawls on granite walls.
There is no light here, but I can see.

Silence spirals through quiet corridors.
Memory crackles, pops.
There is no fire here, but I am warm.

Silhouettes sink beneath shadows,
Ash grey, growing, exposed wound.
There is no light here, but I can see.

Golden faces stare at polished walls,
White-hot words in flame.
There is no fire here, but I am warm.

Where the forest fell, grass grows deep.
Around eyes, home looking back at home.
There is no light here, but I can see.

We built it here to set the earth ablaze.
Smoldering, these twelve stone doors remain.
There is no fire here, but I am warm.
There is no light here, but I can see.

Greetings

I want to say "Thank you."
Thank you for the bread,
the salt, and the wine.

I want to say "I see you"
in crowds of shape-shifting students,
your face like a lantern.

I want to say "I know you."
I wait in anticipation
to see what vast ocean you will cross.

I want to say that I am impossibly
woven to you,
but, instead, I'll say "Howdy"
and hope you understand.

Midnight Yell

Every Midnight Yell
I stand just outside the stadium and listen.

From a distance it sounds
like the ocean, pushing voices.

I hear my mother visiting, her hair in a bob,
my cousin seven years ago.

I hear them hovering around the YMCA,
filling up the Grove.

I hear those asleep and those arising.

I hear you and the one that took your place,
standing still in the audible tide.

And when the canon fires
and the lights go out,
I think that, for a moment,

we are all awake.

The other education

Today I learned about the heart
how its four chambered house pushes
blood through our body like a carnival ride,
how roller-coaster and merry-go-round we are.

                    Today I learned about the heart,
                    how we must hold it like glass, but
                    use it like granite, how its
                    epileptic beat is a calling.

Today I learned about gravity,
how because we are so spinning
we're sewn to the ground like buttons
by elastic, law-abiding thread.

                    Today I learned about gravity,
                    how heavy some words can be,
                    how "alone" climbs the branch of your neck,
                    and with great simian arms, pulls ground.

Today I learned about economics,
how we're tied on these lines
like catfish, how we are simultaneously gathering
pebbles and flinging them to the sea.

                    Today I learned about economics,
                    how the more numerous the stars,
                    the less we will sacrifice to touch one,
                    how with too many heavens, a god is not just.

Today I learned that
these classrooms are getting smaller,
these lessons, easier to chew.

                              Today I learned
              these classrooms are getting bigger,
                  these lessons, harder to swallow.

Muster

"Here" sits
Somewhere between reverence and apology
Rolling unwanted from mourning mouths
As if,
To claim their presence here
Is to claim their absence there,
A weight
Some haven't the strength to bear.
So we,
The walls,
Have come to see them through.

Now forming

In harvest rows of wheat and blood
they stand as farmer soldiers, who
with weapons drawn, approach the field
commanded as a man, a man
whose only duty is to sing
of those who came to battle here.

While thirsty soldiers hold to hear
a courtly call to arms, the blood
beneath hot skin begins to sing,
to twitch, to crawl up veins of those who
would, if necessary, man
an empty station on the field.

The men then walk inside the field
of eyes and tongues that ache to hear
the brass, the drums, the pulse of men
who play by sheets of seraphed blood,
who learned the notes by watching those who
first made heavy maces sing.

At once, the weapons wielded sing
a song across the threaded field.
The soldiers' shoulders flash like grain. Who
sees this ocean salt and sand hears
weathered waves roll thick like blood,
blood dripping from a breathing man,

and on the waves, we'll take this man,
his hands held high as if to sing
a note for every drop of blood
that falls to water turgid field,
a stone field full of those who here
have shown us who is held by whom.

We'll watch them glide like ice, like air, who
poised as buildings, bricks of men,
will rise and raze small empires here,
and soldiers still will bravely sing
the song we know in the furrowed field,
we irrigate with our best blood.

Only the blood of those who
walked this field as noble men
will hear their song sung here.

Century Tree

They told me if I
walked beneath her
canopy alone, I
would die alone.

Years later, as
I sit on her carved bench
and imagine that
each leaf is a memory
and each branch is a person,

I can't imagine anyone
is alone here. The cool
Brazos wind picking up —
the roots below,
holding us all together.

Almost a century

Almost a century of cookies
of cookbooks full of family
of thimble and thread and sewing circles
of denim and lace, vests and pins
of goodies and grab bags

Almost a century of Christmas vacations
of Easter, Thanksgiving
of holding adults
that, for the moment, still feel like children

Almost a century of women
of meetings and dinner parties
of raffles and banquets
of graduations, Musters, Silver Taps,
of Final Reviews
of weekends spent remembering

Almost a century of college
of boys asking about laundry and girls
of girls asking about laundry and boys
of crying phone calls
of laughing phone calls
of no phone calls
of hands held tight, knelt down
in some dark room praying

Almost a century of mothers
Holding a four-year breath

Authority

I've seen yell leaders on the field,
white suits and winsome smiles,
passing it back to the county line.

I've seen them silence stadiums
with wave of their hand. Hold fans
in a fist.

I've watched them lead us through "Aggieland"
their arms a metronome,
their faces ever forward,
their voices firing like a canon.

They are, to be sure,
princes of the moment.

But,
>when their shadows are painted
>on field or façade,
>when the shape of their bodies
>stretch seven-fold,
>
>I can't help but focus
>on what can't possibly be shadows,
>but instead, silhouettes
>of the men just behind them,

those farmers who first taught us to fight.

The candle
In memory of Jeff Wetuski '91

On a high shelf in my cousin's bedroom,
between the trophies and signed baseballs,
a Muster candle sits, unlit.

It sits where it has sat
for the last twenty-four years
gathering dust.

I was ten when it
lit up a quiet room,
full of quiet faces.

Now, each time I sit
in the silence of Muster,
I think about the day
that candle was glowing,

how my aunt must have cried,
how my uncle's hands trembled,

how absent they must have felt
when the crowd answered "Here."

Bonfire remembrance 2009

They flood in, small rivers
these families and students
who did not see Bonfire burn like a canopy,
did not hear Bonfire laugh like a harlequin,
did not feel Bonfire, shaking and shuddering.

here in this place that now echoes a memory
quiet hymns hum in the halls of our history.

Now is the night when their open ears, listening
quiet enough for a ten- tear-old voice

to say, "Silence young soldiers, our work is not over here.
Patience my brothers and sisters, still smoldering.

"We are the smoke and the ashes, the wind
that has yet to die down, that will stir through these logs

"Until you and your progeny, you with our history, you
in your destiny,
set stones ablaze."

This ring — a cinquain

this ring
will sew my skin
to you, thick thread of our
fathers, this university
a loom

this ring
will out run my
blood and breath till one day
this golden stone will rest its weight
on bone

Weight

Boots shuffle, high heels scrape, tennis shoes slide.
Flip flops flip then flop in a silent pilgrimage.

Shadows are greeted by the shifting and shaping crowds.
Welcoming strangers carve an open space.

Someone across the plaza coughs.
A man to my left breathes heavy breaths.
A couple is whispering.

Somewhere, far away, bells ring.
The tune is familiar, warm, calming.

The percussion of a corps outfit drums against the sidewalk.
The uniforms give the hour a little more authority,
A little more honor,
A little more weight.

"Amazing Grace" peals from the bell tower.
People are thinking about God,
About home,
About friends,
About class,
About future,
About God and home.

Headlights flash, the train screams, someone else coughs.
Several people whisper, "Bless you."
It's a time to be holy.
The last bell chimes.

Silence brings daydreamers back to attention.
The crowd holds its breath.... then POP,
POP,
> POP,
>> POP.

Their cadence firecrackers, flaring up with sound.
They pace the heartbeats,
Pace the breaths.
Inhale, POP.
Exhale, POP.
They glow like ghosts against the charcoal drawing of a four storied tomb.

They move like liquid.

The Ross Volunteers crackle in perfect rhythm against the cold concrete
They blow towards the old man shouting light back at the moon.

Hold, then POP.

The time between steps gives the other senses time to sense.
Its cold, my legs hurt, the crowd shifts its weight.
It smells like perfume, vanilla, and cigarettes.

POP

As I strain to listen, I hear commands

Muffled by the weight of the moment.

The ghosts are a well-oiled machine.
A phantom fleet dripping though perfectly synchronized acts of contrition.
Their movements are deliberate, regretful,
As circumstance forces then to perform their well-rehearsed routine.

Guns down .
Guns up.
Turn.
POP.
Guns down.
Guns up.

The slow hum of one voice moves the specters through calculated motions,
Then, with an automated whisper,
Before silence folds itself,

SLAM.
The walls of penitent hush crash.
Birds scatter from still shaking trees
Desperate to find sanctuary from respect's cacophony
The sound echoes through the empty tomb.
Hearts stop, breaths stop, thoughts stop.
There is a heavy pause,

Then all simultaneously regain rhythm.

The second wave of guns comes with less surprise.

SLAM.

2000 shoulders shiver.
A girl to my right whispers the Lord's Prayer.
A boy to my left checks his phone.

He feels the wait, but has yet to feel the weight.

SLAM.
You can separate the sound and the light,
Holding each in a hand.

Somewhere, in the darkness, in the stretched mouth of time,
Three buglers play.

The first notes are the heaviest.

Heads bow, knees bend, chests cave.
Finding it difficult to hold up beneath the weight.
The air becomes thick.

Another unwanted headlight reveals the blond hair of the girl in front of me.
I think I have a class with her.
Maybe that's a different girl.
Maybe she couldn't come tonight.

Maybe her parents came instead.

The sounds pour like a river through the crowds,
Washing them,
Cleansing them,
Drowning them.
I come up for breath, then the bugles start again.

This time I'm focused,
Looking hard at the dome
To see if I can see three nameless cadets
Smearing a sigh across 25 notes.

I think about the girl.
I wonder if she's standing on the rotunda,
Tennis shoes on the cold bronze dome.
Can she see who came, who forgot, who decided to forget?

The last beginning steals my attention
Sounds fall like lead snow,
Soft, clean, smothering.

I wait for the last note, always the longest

Watch it rise just to our necks.

As the sound is cut the crowd awakes,
Blinking, shaking the stone off.

The congregation walks slowly until they are sure it's not too early to move,
Then quickly so no one will question if they moved too early.
Some gather around benches drawing bowed head circles.
Some put arms around one another.
Some move.
Some don't.
Some can't.
Their thoughts try to find sea legs.

The plaza empties,
A broken snow globe with students spilling out.
Behind me I can hear the ghosts
Awaken from their slumber.
POP, POP, POP

They vanish in the same zephyr they drifted in on.
The lamps flicker on.

Boots shuffle, high heels scrape, tennis shoes slide.
But one family hasn't moved.
For them this wasn't a moment,
This was momentous.

My stride becomes longer.
People, out of courage or disrespect, start conversation.
We leave the weight at the tomb

With them,
With her,
With honor.

As I walk, the clock tower chimes.
The wind crawls up the trees.
I remember something about an island,
Something about the whole.

Silver Taps revisited

The soldier
tight like wire
on my right

has metal bones
that rattle
in this thin air.

He is brilliant
in the moon,
a quiet, unsettling
sight.

These moments
are understood
in the darker
cupboards of
our kitchens

where we
are not fragments

but a whole,
faceless and wide.

Echo Taps

There is no more honorable
an act than the quiet
night that begs cadets
 into an evening formation,

where two trumpets sing
and none are offered solace.

We have remembrance, and we have grief.
Honor is the highest form of both.

12th Man

We don't stand at sporting
events because we think
we may be called to play;
we stand at sporting events
because we've already been
called.

In college, I played third deck,
I kept hats off during yells,
and reminded freshmen girls
to stay through the fourth quarter.

They've recently moved me to
my living room where, still
standing, I can carefully
synthesize both commentary
and a large pepperoni pizza.

One day I'll get moved to
the west side, 20 rows up
at the fifty yard line, I'll
watch the student section
sway. I won't have words.

That will be my position,
a necessary part of the team.

The promise

My favorite tradition is not
the Aggie Ring, though I love
the way it makes us tremble.

It is not Reveille, though she
would be a worthy choice.

My favorite tradition is not
Muster or Midnight Yell, not
the Century Tree or the Century Club.

I do not think Silver Taps
or the 12th Man is what defines us.

My favorite tradition grows each year.
They pour into this town like marbles.

They are terrified and overwhelmingly brave.

My favorite tradition is not an act;
it is the promise that tomorrow
all we love will still be here.

My Experience

My scrapbook

I never kept a scrapbook in college,
no boxes of loose pictures,
no ink-heavy journal.

When I remember,
it's as simple as a memory.

I kissed a girl in that parking lot
during a light rain.

I played bones on those benches
when Bonfire still burned.

That building is where I had my first class,
American History, 8:00 am.

I lay on that stone for an entire afternoon,
watching clouds pass.

I have a memory for every statue and sidewalk,
every bench and tree,

and when I walk across this campus
I hear pages turn.

Writing process

I'm collecting these poems like cranes,
flying back to where they were folded,
where the wind blew them from my arms.

I'm adjusting these poems like so many lenses,
focusing on the minute minutes,
twisting my eye like a Stevenson character.

I'm filing these poems like taxonomy,
decorating each one with dead Latin,
asking them nervously to stand still while I count.

I am weighing these poems like cantaloupe
using balance beam hands to hold
both them and the memory they're worth.

I'm cutting these poems like nails
trying hard not to rip them with my teeth,
no one wants blood at the cuticle.

I'm writing these poems like a ghost,
head full of faces, staring in foggy windows,
writing my words on the glass.

About to leave these halls

I wonder what it would be like, a freshman again,
ever so gently slipping out of the stretched skin of high school.

As I packed my first box I would grab the yearbook off the shelf,
my prom picture, and some unread play or book of poetry.

As I sifted through my closet I would color-code and fold t-shirts
pretending my college career would be this ordered, this predictable.

I would drive by my old high school, with its heavy doors
and white floors, twist tight the top of every bottle.

If I were about to start over, I would set my life between my thumb and forefinger,
Hold it up to the light, and squint to see the stitches.

I wouldn't sleep the night before I left.

Instead, my mind would race with the regal faces, empty thrones,
And the un-held scepters of a campus where I could become king.

Composites

These brothers know more than my name,
the weight of my blood.
They know me.
They stand, surrounding me, palms open,
not to push, but hold me steady
like one would a rocking vessel.
They are within reach of me,
defining me, refining me,
helping me stand on these straw legs.

They talk with a hand on my shoulder,
carrying conversation like cups of water;
careful, concerned with each drop.
These brothers know what a responsibility I am.

These brothers follow and lead me,
walk beside me.

They are in tuxedos on my wedding day,
next to me at little league games,
helping me find pieces when I break,
sitting patient
while glue dries.

These brothers will play chess
on a warped wooden table.
They'll sit quietly to watch suns set.

They'll have a gift beneath my tree
wrapped by my children.

These brothers will shuffle in suits,
carrying me,
kissing my wife,
shaking my grown son's hand,
teaching him to be the man
they taught me to be.

Fellow students

Sometimes when I walk across campus
I think of how many times my path
crosses the memory of yours,
sharing footsteps.

When I sit on a bench
I wonder how many people reading this
have sat beside me, not knowing
I would arrive years later.

When I touch the side of a building
I wonder who last shared same-space
with my hand, catching themselves from a fall,
feeling how rough the granite is.

In the grass I think that, maybe,
it remembers the weight of your body,
how you lay here next to me on a picnic,
on a day much like today

then walked back to your dormitory,
and lying still on your mattress,
thought about what other students
still stand silent in your room.

Passing the torch

I think it is not a passing of the torch
as much as it is a torching of the past.
And as I sit here, ash-eyed and forgotten,
as the chronal flames leap beneath my chin,
I am whole and human and combustible,
and this scream I sing is not one of pain
but one of longing and hope and light.

On turning 19

As professors, we feel older than most people our age. We say that we choose our profession because it keeps us young, but the liver spots, the failing eyes, and our sore backs are constant reminders that though we may feel it, we are, in fact, not young. We are distinguished, aged, experienced, and a slew of other euphemisms that belie our envious souls.

Today one of my students turned 19.

19 is a high school novel to me, picked up once every few years and wedged back on the shelf between Wuthering Heights and The Jungle. A book I never read during those formative years. A story I cannot put down.

19 is an unnamed port I once tasted at a party. It is the hundred bottles I have since had, trying, once again, to find it. It is the color, the weight, the wood, and the fruit. The cup of my tongue, the stem of my throat.

19 is an open field. There are no trees, no people, no animals, and no memories. There is only the affirming reality of the grass beneath me, the open-mouthed imagination of the sky above, and the sweet air I breathe somewhere in between.

Today one of my students turned 19.

I said, "Happy Birthday," with a smile.

But he doesn't know I'd just as soon cut him if I thought he might bleed time.

Waiting

On roofs with cigars
Outside the storm
The sky a light
God dripping
Down the windshield,
I told you I would
Come if I was called.

In bars with beers
Balanced on felt beds
Darts like daggers
Motionless in air
I told you I would
Come if I was called.

At midnight pacing
Pavement, hyphenated highways
Leading us in and out
Of hometown heroism
I told you I would
Come if I was called.

Days before deliverance
Heavily creased gowns
In pre-packaged plastic,
Empty frames being filled
I told you I would
Come if I was called.

Decades dripped through
Ringed fingers, both smooth
Small hands and silent mornings
Before the dawn
Behind the sky
I told you I would
Come if I was called.

Grown men glowing
Umbrella legged
And brilliant
Wading through winters
Like so many rivers
I told you I would
Come if I was called.

On roofs with cigars
Inside the storm
The sky alit
God dripping
Down the windshield
I told you I would come.

Souvenirs

What I'll take with me won't hang on my wall, staring at
itself in glass, gold-stamped skin to
>   remind me of long gowns and shaking hands.

What I'll take with me won't fit on a finger, wound
filigree full of symbolism and salt, making
>   me feel heavy-handed.

What I'll take with me won't fill up a résumé, black,
12-point font on wrinkle free parchment, a
>   bulleted autobiography.

What I'll take with me won't settle in a pitcher,
>   won't get shaken in a 42 game,
>   won't be standing on third deck.

What I'll take with me, I won't know I took until I find it
years later in the pocket of some
>   unworn coat.

Then I'll sit, staring at it for hours, thinking of home.

Close
for Eva

Tonight, my niece tells me,
the moon is closer than normal.

A learned seven-year-old, she attempts
to explain some elementary astrophysics,

but her oration on planetary motion
is cut short by my sister's offer of ice cream.

And while tomorrow's greatest astronomer
does a quick conical volume calculation

to see if her younger sister has more strawberry
swirl than she, my eyes are drawn back

to the moon and its pock-marked complexion.
It looks heavy in the helium sky, a ball,
a balloon, a plate, an egg. Also, a marshmallow,
an eye, a pregnant spider, those metaphors
with which we are less familiar:

a cup of milk, a snow crab, a blanched olive,
an uncovered knee, a hole, a bald man in prayer.

As my nieces spin and slide on their linoleum
kitchen floor, I step out into the Tennessee night.
I reach my hand into the cool mid-March breeze.

I stretch my fingers as far as they will go,
knowing that tonight I am as close as I have
ever been to touching the moon with all its brightness.

And depending on the next steps of sweet Eva
and the incredible gravity of strawberry swirl, it may be
the closest I'll ever come.

Yesterday

I have folded the days
of last year like small
paper cranes.

I have thrown them
by handfuls into
the windy night

and watched them
make starry circles
in the frozen sky.

Since they left, I have
searched bare branches
and open fields

but have found no
paper wing or still-
flapping day.

They must have joined
their brothers and sisters,
perched high

in an eternal tree
whose leafless branches
are white with our history.

Non-reg's lament

I admire the Corps of Cadets,
Their polished brass,
Polished tongues.
I admire their starched uniforms and posture,
Their sharp biders and turns,
Heavy boots, heavy stares.

I admire the Corps of Cadets
The way I admire the jagged head of Everest,
Standing at a distance,
Unable to feel how cold and regal it is
So high above the sea.

Preparation
for Henry Gerecke 2022

We're still building in blocks
what you'll come home to,
still sitting in circles with sewing needles.
We've got scissors and glue,
      bricks and mortar,
          a handful of hands, and a pocket watch.

We've got people pushing up the trees
      a few inches a year.
We've got people pulling on our corners,
      stretching out the kingdom.

Loose ends have been tongue-tied,
and the rugs are 12 feet high.

We've got problems we've been cutting into pieces,
33, easy-to-clean, non-toxic pieces.

Your crown is in Koldus,
your robe in Evans,
and your throne is three feet above Albritton.

We're still building in blocks
what you'll come home to,
but we'll be ready.

Just keep banging your drums.
Keep marching around the house.

We'll hold your place.

Before the game

shake them like a priestess
an oracle
a soothsayer
twist them in your cauldron
hemlock
whatnot
wash them on a wooden table
ivory shells
cedar sand

roll the skeletons

but bones will fall
like bones

Simply put
for the men of 1006 Holik

In the simplest of metaphors, we
are nine forks of a branch that's dividing
in complex dimensions, the lengths
and directions we stretch are unknown.
We are reaching barked fingers and handfuls
of leaves into air, into sky,
into clouds, and we're roasting them hot
on a campfire, dressing in smoke.

In the simplest of metaphors, we
are nine heads of a hydra whose god-
man in training can't cut quick enough
to keep nine angry necks from re-growing
nine fiercesome white fifty-toothed smiles,
and in cutting our collars he lights
liquid fires. We bloom red atomic.
We flower in shrapnel. We sing.

In the simplest of metaphors, we
are nine harts on the ridge of a mountain,
slow moving and sacred, whose blankets
of winter hang heavy beneath
our black hooves. We sit quiet like books.
We hold court on the crowns of our rock
candelabra, light fires with bone
as the kindling, our antlers the wood.

In simplest of similes, we
are like brothers, like fathers, like suns.

Goodbye

Tonight I said goodbye to
College Station. On my way
home from a short run, a late
night train blocked my path.

Uncharacteristically patient, I sat
down and watched the heavy
machinery roll by. It was there
in the spinning and the cranking,
in the squealing and the growling,
that I began to say goodbye.

I put my memories in a
small brown box that I'd been
saving. I dog-eared the top
like my mother taught me.

I packed up my scholarly books
and let my fiction and poetry
fly away on its paperback wings.
It was a beautiful migration.

I left pens and pencils in
my desk, sure that new ink
and lead would suit me better,
wherever I was going.

I took heavy breaths as I
systematically said farewell to

the buildings, the windows, the trees,
the benches, and the fountains of
this little make-believe village.

Then, finally, as the train rumbled
and shook the ground beneath me,
I looked up and said goodbye.
It did not stop to respond.

I stood up, crossed the tracks,
and continued my run, knowing
I was no longer going home,
but instead, going to the place
I will forever be from.

a special thanks

To Robert Carpenter '12, who selflessly devoted himself to this project, who pulled the poems off the shelf, and who through creativity and skill wove this all together. A stranger until a few months ago, Robert agreed, as most Aggies would, to help lend a hand. His direction, insight and dedication are the only reasons this book has been completed. Our brief but productive collaboration is doubly rich as it has produced a product and a profundity: the product — the book in your hands; the profundity — that we are never too old to make new Aggie friends.